Winter Beach

John Hallam Lott

WebVivant Press

www.webvivantpress.com

First published 2017

Copyright © John Hallam Lott 2017

The right of John Hallam Lott to be identified as the author has been asserted in accordance with the UK Copyright, Design and Patents Act 1988.

All rights reserved: no part of this publication may be reproduced, stored in a retrieval system, or transmitted in any form or by any means, electronic, mechanical, photocopying, recording, or otherwise without the prior written permission of the Author. This book may not be lent, resold, hired out or otherwise disposed of by way of trade in any form of binding or cover other than that in which it is published without the prior written consent of the Author.

Global Edition

ISBN: 978-1-908708-05-2

Published by WebVivant Press

www.webvivantpress.com

~

Contents

Preface	5
Winter beach	7
Swallows	9
Waiting	11
Buzzard	13
The red shoes	15
The question	16
Dinner	17
Mule tracks	19
Such sweet sorrow	21
Before the roar	22
Heatwave	23
Summer beach	25
Finality	27
The wood carver	29
Autumn	30
Olae Europeae	31
The time traveller's lament	33
Paris	34
Memories	37
Salobrena dig	38
Disappointment	41
The bar	42
Ships that collide in the night	43
Yuletide	44
The people have spoken	47
Oh dear!	48

Cover image and photographs on pgs. 6, 10, 14, 20, 32, 36 and 46 by Steve Mansfield-Devine (www.zolachrome.com).

All illustrations and photograph on pg.24 by Minnie Lott.

Sculpture on pg.28 by Laurie Emberson.

Preface

Poetry is experiencing something of a popular revival and it is interesting to speculate why this should be so. Rap, the anarchic face of poetry, although none the less viable for that, is one obvious example although it could be argued that Rap is a genre whose appeal is aimed at a specific audience, whereas poetry should have an appeal which is universal.

Another reason, perhaps, why poetry is being read and listened to more has something to do with the changes in language, resulting from the culture of modern usage. 'Techno-speak' and texting are forms of communication from which all emotion and imagery have been drained. As a means of communicating information it works well but that is all it does. It does not 'speak' in the way that poetry does, suggesting pictures and rhythms that evoke chords of recognition in the recipient. There exists within most of us, a need to understand more of our human condition and, through the centuries, writers have used the medium of poetry in an attempt to further this understanding.

This collection of poetry has attempted to cover some of these points and ranges from the emotional, to the metaphysical and to those inspired by images and observation.

Winter beach

Its bed of soiled sand stripped,
The sea has retreated almost to an horizon
Blurred by bitter winds and lowering clouds.
Those who choose to brave these chilling wastes are few.
Some red faced joggers.
Wellied walkers exercising dogs confused
By too much space and too many smells.
Mostly, though, it is the shellfish gatherers.
Specks now in the distant shallows,
Clutching their buckets, rakes and trowels,
They have braved the icy elements
And marched resolutely through the mollusc midden
Of the dry sands to their favoured grounds.
A free meal, be it razor clams, mussels or cockles,
A bi-valve bonanza lies out there for the taking
And will be harvested for the freshest of fish suppers.
Salty juices mopped up with a crisp baguette
And all washed down with a wine tart enough to make the teeth curl.
Yet further out, the kite-surfers,
Their jazzy colours alien to this grey world and veiled by spray,
Buck and bounce their rubber-clad forms
In an ecstasy of wet-suited abandonment.
Behind the promenade, shuttered villas blind until Easter,
Rest wrapped and muffled against the return of the waves
While absentee landlords, cocooned in Parisian offices,
Think only of sun-soaked sand and balmy beach picnics.
They give not a thought to the almost empty,
Silent, wind-blown beauty of their winter beach.

Swallows

They perch on overhead wires like choirs of agitated nuns.
Preening their miniature scimitar wings
And practising their scales.
We see them and are seized by a seasonal sadness.
That time of year again, when days perceptibly shorten
And we are reminded of the mortality of passing time.
We rejoice at their arrival, the promise of lingering warmth,
A sun bursting summer of sweet scented mornings
And evenings which go on for ever.
Aperitif in hand, we watch them feed
Like demented acrobats,
Skimming, soaring and slicing their way
Through the pre-dusk buttermilk sky.
Not for much longer though.
Now they are replete and prepared for the long haul.
Spending more time on the wires and less on the wing.
Soon the last will have left,
Leaving us behind to face the colourful uncertainties of autumn
And the certain chill of winter.
Until next year, when eager voices proclaim
The first sighting of the first swooping swallow of summer.

Waiting

She waits in the middle of a bleak floor
Of a large impersonal restaurant
At the top of a smart department store.
She stands,
Hands clasped in front of her,
Dulled eyes scanning the tables.
She would like to be waiting for an elegant man of means
But she isn't.
She is just waiting to take orders from anybody,
Anybody at all!
She is not old and quite beautiful, in a disappointed sort of way.
She wanted to be a dancer
Or a teacher
Or the wife of one of those men for whom she would like to be waiting.
A successful man who would bring her here to shop
For smart exciting clothes
And here, to the restaurant, for an aperitif perhaps.
Sadly, she had no sense of rhythm, was not very bright
And fell pregnant at fifteen.
Now she stands the stance of the defeated,
Knowing that her youth, her fragile loveliness
Is trickling out of her like sand through an hourglass.
Not quite, anymore, the perfect posture,
The defiant tilt of the chin,
The "I will if you will" challenge in her eyes.
The make-up is a little heavier,
The shoes more comfortable.
But she is a good waitress
Who does what she is told and is reasonably honest.
She will keep her job but not her derelict, dusty dreams.

Buzzard

I see you perched, prouder than a peacock
On a wire, mundane but for the myriad messages
That pass beneath your feet.
Your back straight, your eye commanding countryside contours
That fall outside my meagre range of vision.
Suddenly, my wind-screened view is filled
Dramatically, spectacularly by your passing.
Is it a game to leave your launch so late?

Were I that small furry creature,
Cowering under tussocks and fearing all
But those whose power does not exceed my own,
My instincts would anticipate my death
By a vengeful Valkyrie.
As it is, I cannot help but marvel how such cruelty
Could be so exquisitely packaged
And when I see you balletic in the blue above
And hear your keen and keening cry of love,
I find myself enraptured of a raptor
Whose razored talons tear and tease at my emotions.

The red shoes

A siesta heat hangs over the parched plaza
Like a lazy shroud.
My coffee, black and thick as treacle
Is suspended short of its first electric sip,
When I see those bright red shoes
Cut across that sun-seared square
Like an original thought.
From the shadow of my sheltered patio
I wondered, why so red
When the rest of your dress is so undeniably drab.
An act of defiance?
Did he say, dismissively, "You're wearing those with that?"
And was it lost on him, your spirited riposte.
"I am wearing these red shoes because
They are the most exciting thing in a world
Which you have made mundane."

~

Perhaps they were a gift, given in love
And you wanted him to see you wearing
His adoration on your feet.
Perhaps they are the only pair that you possess.
If that is so, I would want you to know
That you are regally defined by the shade of those shoes.
Your steps register a faint flamenco hammer
As you walk, head high, back straight as a picador's lance.
You near the corner.
Another moment of our unconscious lives about to disappear.
I stir my regret into my cooling coffee
And put my scarlet-fevered imagination back to sleep.

The question

She gripped my arm and whispered "Why?"
He looked away.

The day was clear, sapphire bright and fresh as innocence,
As, indeed, were they,
Young and newly minted from their Uni.
Could she bring him on a trip to France, she'd asked.
Together, they'd laughed and chatted in the car,
Confident of their immortality, their world unclouded by doubt.

Arriving, the sun shone obscenely on the site we had come to view.
Everything so pristine,
Perfection, under a sky of perfect blue.
It took them a moment to realise where they were and what it was.
No sound but the respectful hum of mowers, manicuring faultless lawns
And, behind us, incoming waves tirelessly scouring the sullied sands.
Before us, fanned out with geometric formality,
Ten thousand marble memorials.
Weepingly white, quartz crystals winking brazenly at the sun.

They stepped back. So much death, such a beautiful day.
They looked at me, at each other and walked slowly to the first row.
Read the carved inscriptions.
He held out a hand, she clasped it, desperately.
They moved along, first one line, then the next
Until they had seen enough to learn that mortality takes no account of age.
They returned to where I stood, aching for their vulnerability.

She gripped my arm and whispered "Why?"
He looked away.

Dinner

A corner table, by a window misted with steam
From a kitchen small, even for this cut-price cafe.
Early evening and people pass oblivious to all but
Each other and the links of family, love or friends.
Their eyes, casually sweep over the panel of opaque glass
Seeing nothing, but the haloed lights
Adding their cold cheer to the stark interior.
But there she sits, her gaze bouncing off the clouded glaze.
Alone in this city teeming with life, of which she has no part.
As the passing shapes come in and out of her focus,
She conjures sharper visions of lovers, mothers and others
Who share an intimacy from which she is excluded.
She toys with the food on her plate,
But the reassuring wine is never far from her restless hand.
She drains her glass, pays her bill and leaves.
Swallowed by the city, she finds her anonymous apartment,
Opens her door and another bottle
And settles down to another evening with her thoughts.

Mule tracks

Mule tracks,
Intractable as mules and old as time,
Meander through groves of olive green and citrus yellow.
Lined with walls built dry
And paved with stones that challenge the stoutest of souls
And the stoutest of soles.
Ankle-wrenching flints, knee-numbing granites
Time-hardened by centuries of sun and a million dainty hooves.
The paths twist and turn,
Rise and fall, embracing terraces from which countless generations
Have scraped, tilled and toiled to stay alive.
Permanently precarious, traditionally tamed,
The tracks serve settlements neglected by roads
But remembered by itinerant herders, indolent donkeys
And hardened hikers.
The drum of car wheels on distant metalled highways
Harmonises with the busy buzz of bees on the gorse-dotted tracks
And walkers march to the music of hums, ancient and modern.

Such sweet sorrow

It pains me to say that it's over
But I fear it's a final goodbye
Perhaps, in the hazy future, we might rediscover
Something of the pleasure enjoyed this time around
But I think that unlikely.
Brief though our acquaintance has been,
I have valued every moment spent in your company.
For you have given me the precious gift of laughter.
You have exercised my imagination
And sometimes caused me a momentary
Stab of pain.
You have sustained me through some dark days
And diverted me from troubled thoughts.
Taking you to bed has always been a particular pleasure.
But now it is over.
It is time to turn over a new leaf,
Start another chapter.
For you will be banished from my life to the over-full shelf of memories.
And although I might grieve for a moment,
As a promiscuous bibliophile
I am already anticipating the next encounter
And the plot that awaits me therein.

Before the roar

Early morning cities unfurl like fresh, green leaves.
The raucous clamour of fun-fuelled hedonism is stilled
And arterial lungs are decongested.
This is the time, a special time
When the stones gently wake to a subdued symphony
Of cleaners and licentious cats tip-toeing home.
Sad cardboard-carpeted doorways still embrace their fragile cargoes
And the ghosts of yesterday's footsteps vanish with the dewy dawn.
Early breakfasts flavour the chill air
While Greasy Spoon servers, whistling quietly to themselves,
Eye the lightening sky
Before committing their rusty furniture to the fresh-swilled flags.
Early shift coppers wink their good mornings to night shift nurses.
Dogs sniff out the old and the new,
Their owners pulled from pillar to post, furtive fingers
Grasping hopeful little plastic bags.
This is the time, a special time,
Before the gaping subterranean passages disgorge their hordes
Of workers, shoppers, tourists, tat-sellers and transits.
Before the air is blue with car-carried curses
And bus-borne badinage.
Before the tills tick, the keyboards clatter and the money takes over.
Before all that. Now! This special time.
Anticipation hovers over the streets like a benevolent presence
And the city prepares to enfold its stretched, waking arms around itself.

Heatwave

Sandalled soles crackle over dead, dry grass.
Shimmering mirages hover over black satin tarmac.
Cattle and sheep munch morosely on yellowing fodder
And huddle pointlessly under listless branches.
The buzzy world of insects is loud with industry
And swallows swerve and sweep at the end of another sated day.

~

Children, noisy in their alfresco freedom,
Jump in and out of pools, grazing knees and elbows
On the unforgiving and un-watered flinty ground.
The skies, blue from horizon to heaven,
Are criss-crossed by skeins of vapour trails
As town-tired workers, budget-booked
And sardine-packed, make their pilgrimages
To worship the same sun but in another place.

~

No rain now for weeks and weeks.
Shrubs shrivel, borders burn and gardeners groan.
Spiders gratefully spin their silken threads
In lazy loops of hopeless hoses,
Abandoned and banned by local decree.
Pollen proliferates: eyes itch, noses run
And producers of anti-this and anti-that
Grow fat on the fears of peeling people.
Through those long, dark days of winter
We longed for summer sunlight but now,
A little rain, preferably at night,
Would make us feel so much better.

Summer beach

Thronged by a thong-sandalled host of happy people,
The sundrenched beach is a hive
Of activity and passivity, age dividing one from the other.
The very young and the very old sleep in parasoled shade,
While lovers view each other's bodies with a desire
Uncomplicated by lust.
Toddlers toddle and dig; fathers eager to display their skills,
Toil with bucket and spade.
Keep-fitters stretch, bend and perform their callisthenics
At the surf's edge, through which would-be swimmers
Plod relentlessly towards an acceptable depth.
Then, suddenly, movement ceases.
Time stands still as a small girl invades the scene.
Four, or five, she commands attention out of all proportion to her size.
Clothed, not in jeans or swimwear, she wears a dress.
White and decorated with ribbons and bows.
Not too ornate but simple and timeless.
In that instant, the sun shines
Only for her.
She casts her spell and there is a moment of magic
As all activity becomes distant and remote
And the boisterous clamour of beach-born bonhomie recedes into silence.
It is as if she has been transported from an earlier age
And as she stands motionless,
Her eyes fixed on a tiny white sail on the far horizon,
The hot sands are frozen into a moment of beauty.

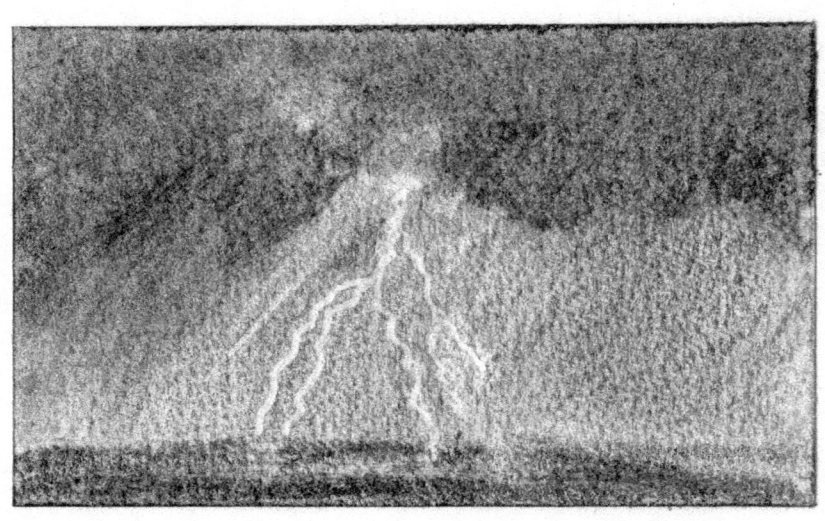

Finality

Think of loneliness.
Then think of the word "alone."
They sound similar and yet, are so very different.
"Alone" can be an elective decision
While loneliness cannot and it is this which defines me.
For I am rejected by all other species,
I am a forgotten fragment of the past
And my precarious presence on this planet unacknowledged
By man.
But why should he?
After all, it is he who has hunted me for fun and for food.
For his profit, he destroyed my habitat, my source of life.
And having done so, he has forgotten me.
Yet I remain, the last, the very last.
I am not alone by choice
And I search in vain to replicate my race.
But my race is run.
My gene pool is drained dry.
And I am
EXTINCT.

The wood carver

A bleak block of raw timber,
Sits heavy on its anchoring plinth.
Promising nothing but an idea,
Buried deep within its heart of oak.
The rude exterior of a chrysalis, within which
The dormant germ of his imagination
Awaits transmutation
Into an object of form and grace.
His blades, sharp as wit, wait while he ponders
The mysteries of grain, of heartwood and pith,
Then as he works, wasted wood reveals the embryo within.
Decades of growth rings rejuvenate
Into tensions of tendon and muscle.
Subtleties of expression, of ecstasy and pain
Are whittled, traced and teased from the reluctant host.
Clinical callipers create proportion
While the natural stress of splitting timber
Is tempted into empathetic form.
The wooden womb yields up a new life
And that which once was rooted and immovable,
Now moves with re-awoken energy.
Abused by chisel, saw and blade,
The aboreal bruising is finally caressed and smoothed,
Oiled and massaged, until the carver's creation,
Liberated at last, stands free in its renaissance.

Autumn

The forest is on fire again.
Slow burning leaves
Of red and gold and orange, licking
And flaming tips of grieving branches.
Slowly, so slowly they twist and curl
In the agony of their dying
Until, releasing their hold on life,
They fall gently, drifting down with unbearable decorum.

On the unrelenting ground they lie,
A multicoloured carpet for passing, senseless feet,
While looming over them,
The trees stand starkly sentinel,
Guarding their dyed, dead, departed decoration.

Olae Europeae

Methuselah was younger than me when he died
But he was merely a figment of biblical fancy
While I am rooted in the reality of stony soil.
I have seen so much history, you wouldn't believe it.
Philosophers, toga-clad, resolved their rhetoric
As they turned their thoughts around my adolescent limbs.
Boabdil rested his sad frame against my trunk
And pondered his imminent capitulation with a sigh
So profound, it reverberated through the centuries.
My bark has been fouled by the blood of fighting men
And, at my feet, lovers have surrendered
To the sweet musk of summer madness.
The boy, seeking shade for his flock,
Has serenaded me with mournful pipe.
Hopeful girls, holding hot hands in a ring,
Have danced a dance of aeonian urgency
To feel a fraction of my natural fertility.
Without the pressings of my fruit
Cultures would have lacked the light to record their wisdom,
Nor warmth to flex their fingers as they wrote.
Myriad cuisines would be bereft
And centuries of human pelts left lustreless and dry.
As indeed, I am now.
Grotesquely formed and gnarled with age extreme,
My canopy, if sparse, leafed still in your favourite green.
Yet, for all my great gifts to man,
I have suffered cruel amputation of my limbs
And year by year, century after century,
Have been beaten for my eternal knowledge.

The time traveller's lament

We have been together a long time now
And I don't like him very much.
All these years, from uncognitive cradle to the present day,
He has been at my side.
When I was a child he kept a very low profile,
Probably preferring the company of others
But as I became older, he started to creep into my consciousness.
Still, for many years, he kept a respectful distance
And the only reminder of his presence
Was the occasional card or letter,
Invariably edged in black.
Now though, now that I have attained an uncertain maturity,
He is with me nearly every day.
In fact, I feel that he is stalking me.
I look over my shoulder, just to check
That he is not treading on my heels or getting too close.
If the ever-decreasing circle of my acquaintances is anything to go by
He is certainly busier than he used to be.
But I am being very careful not to make the mistake
Of letting him think that I am not aware of him.
Because that would be the ultimate hubris
And a terminal error.

Paris

They are stamped by a pedigree of privilege.
As are the long-dead designer labels that they wear.
Not quite as beguiling as when first bespoke,
A little loose here, a little tight there
But the hand stitching still sings of quality.
Their stage, one of the better arrondissements.
Respectful traffic, respectable people.
They meet, mid-morning, where the boulevards meet,
Their rendezvous, a quintessential corner cafe.

He lifts his once rakish fedora and winces
At the pain in his shoulder, timeworn like the hat.
They lean towards each other,
He a hand resting on her arm,
She supported by an antique ebony cane.
Her carefully coiffed head is turned
First this way, then that
And with dry lips he gently touches paper-thin cheeks.

His ring finger swells around a gold band
Of vows made, never kept and long forgotten.
Only their eyes defy decades of time.
Still sparkling with pleasure of meeting and memories.
Same corner but half a century since
Their first frisson-fuelled encounter.
They met alone and almost by accident,
Their espoused, unsuspecting and elsewhere.

Then, with the panache of a plumed Cyrano,
He swept off his hat and she, elevated on eager toes,
Sought the sweet sensuality of his mouth.
Thus was launched fifty years of illicit love.
Waiters, aprons to the floor, looked away
And pretended to clean immaculate tables.

Their successors still sponge a still immaculate table
Before serving the ritual morning cup of chocolate.
As they watch the couple leave and take their separate ways,
The waiters wonder, how long?
How long before one of these gentle relics
Anachronisms in an alien, button-pressing world,
Orders not two but one sad, single mourning cup?

Memories

Sadness seeps out of the rotting timbers
Like sap from a traumatised tree.
Boards bend and groan in the breeze,
Spiders spin relentlessly
And splintered window shards glow red,
Reflecting the sunset of your conscious life.
Once this shed, now so fragile, was the expression of your hopes,
Your refuge against the spirit-shredding
World of commerce, of manic London life.
Set in a garden on a Welsh hillside,
Air to breathe like you wouldn't believe,
This was to be your haven of retirement.
A place to sit and read and think and savour your Rioja,
While those Black Hill views, the thought of which
Sustained you through the maelstrom
Of making your way, go on for eternity.

You, sadly, have not.
You have forgotten what has gone and the present is meaningless.
You have forgotten the pleasure of protecting
Your precious tongue and groove against the Welsh weather.
You have forgotten nearly everything now,
As your mind inexorably closes off the compartments of your past.
The old door creaks as the ghosts of yesterday
Wander in and out at will.
Tools hang rusty and tentacles of invasive ivy
Embrace them with the sort of passion
You once felt for her.
She grieves your loss and your passing into that other world,
A world of nothingness, unsustained by logic and memory.
Sitting in the old decaying porch, the distant hills are misted by her eyes
As she remembers everything that you cannot.

Salobrena dig

A luscious layer cake of stone and sand
Is tenderly deconstructed by the soft-handed men in hard hats.
Each strata delicately brushed apart,
Revealing patterns of cultures
Laid by those who believed their empires would outlive time.
They did not but the stones have lived to tell their stories.
The deepest dig reveals mosaics,
Formal, precise as a legion on parade.
They tell of calf-thonged, sandalled soldiers
Imperiously imposing their metronomic rule on Iberian soil.
Centuries of centurions savoured this, their favoured Hispania Ulterior.
Motives no longer military,
They lingered for the wine, the oil and the soft sun,
Collecting their tributes on these dainty tiles,
Now new-exposed and squinting at the light.

~

After the light comes the darkness of the hordes.
Sweeping away the majesty of Rome with nomadic insouciance.
The bright conceit of figured floor
Is replaced, defaced, by rude animal shelters.
Instant detritus, a foundation for ever more bestial byres.
Visigothic vandalism, devoid of art and beauty, becomes a non-strata,
Impatiently sieved into finer dust by the safety-jacketed crew
Who shake their yellow heads at this lack of tangible legacy.
These cold Germanic tribes used this soft Southern land as a fly tip,
Leaving little of note to adorn the cabinets of modern museums.
Two hundred years of graceless rubble
Greeted the harsh dignity of the Moor
As he swept, scimitar-handed through the new-baptised nation.

~

Once here, they tamed the precious water,
Training it to perform to Allah's music.
Cascades of sun-saturated droplets graced elegant courtyards
Floored by patterns of swirling stone.
Languid pools reflected the palmed fronds of their desert home.

Sea and landscape were captured by subtle keyhole frames
And the harsh rocks softened by tree-shaded African colours.
Contours captured in brick, mimic the sensual curves of Saharan dunes
And oasis fertility is mirrored by motifs of fern and flower.
The Team are men who love to touch time itself
And they are seduced by this, the art of the Maghreb.
Their work, however, is over and the castle's
Kaleidoscopic history is bared to all.
The millennia it took to build this savoury sandwich of time
Can now be recorded as a tourist trophy in the twinkling of an iPhone.

Disappointment

Sex is in the air again
And don't we know it!
Garbed gaudy in orange, yellow, purple and red,
She comes on to you like an eager, hungry whore.
Her warm breath promising you a good time
Just around the corner.
Her acolytes sing their shrill fecund choruses,
Rutting their ruts and mating their mates.
Oh yes! There's not much subtlety about her or her wiles.
She's got it and she flaunts it, does salacious Spring.
And we fall for it every time,
This promise of long, lazy summer days,
Alfresco fare and the slow, roll-over waves
On to some serendipitous, sandy shore.
But beware this siren song of Spring.
She has the habit of leaving you unfulfilled
Just as things are getting good.
Coitus interruptus!
And before the end of April
We are all snowed in and the wicked, wanton land is sterilised by frost.

The bar

Sitting in the bar and looking around me,
I was stabbed by a brief but sharp pain of nostalgia.
Had I really frequented this pub
Which appeared to have changed so little,
Except that I now, among its regulars, felt depressingly mature.
Haunted and harried by ghosts of my distant past,
Against which the company of the one I love above all else,
Could not quite, for that instant, protect me.
I pondered why the "what we were" and the "what we are"
Is bridgeable only by this intensity of longing
For that which can never again be ours.
But then,
Should some fantastic Faustian future be offered to me,
Would I change what I have now for what I had then?
Exchange experience, knowledge, maturity and above all, love
For the uncertainty of the moment,
The frisson of the "first time."
Those ephemeral hangovers and heartaches
Forgotten before they became fully fledged?
I don't think so.
My ambitions have not reduced in scale but broadened.
Perhaps I take a little longer to reach the corners
In order to experience what lies around them
But the need to know is just as urgent as ever.
The zest for challenge remains undiminished by time
As does the windmill-tilting quest for fairness and equality.
No! A tiny fragment of regret is all it was and, as such,
May safely by consigned to the detritus of my past.

Ships that collide in the night

A friendly phrase,
"Sorry, you go first"
Or
"Looks like rain again."
Ordinary words, innocently delivered,
Can change your life.
Can change the lives of many.
Eyes meet, a polite rejoinder, eyes meet again
And hold for that instant too long.
The accidental hand on the arm, lingers for that instant too long
And a conversation starts.
From there it's a short step to
"Let me help you with that,"
"No really, it's not a problem – Oh! All right then."
Another shared eye contact and it's off to the pub for a quick drink.
Just the one, no harm in that – is there?
Right person, wrong time or wrong person, right time?
Or does that depend
On those omitted from this sparkling new arrangement?

Yuletide

Today, gold is unaffordable but frankincense and myrrh?
Amazon, EBay? Could be worth a try but no,
Probably not.
So we celebrated with a champagne
That was better than usual
And a half-decent bottle of claret or two.
Lots of lovely tinselled gifts,
Tiny tokens of starlight crudely added
To a small pine tree, prematurely pulled from its plantation,
Lent a welcome festive glow to our seasonal worship.
We did play some carols because, after all,
What would the Mass be without them?
And we remembered some of the words –
But not always in the order in which they were written.
Better than nothing though. But then again,
Probably not.
A free-range turkey, small but cost-effectively, if prematurely
Plucked from its intensive rearing pen
Was the centrepiece of our late lunch
Or was it an early dinner? Does it matter?
Probably not!
Paper crowns pronounced our regal status for the day.
All kings, regally rooting in our dismembered crackers
For a "have you heard that one?" moment
And fumbling for some unusable trinket,
Produced in some oriental sweat shop.
A small token of irritated rejection,
The trinket, that is, not the sweated labour
Or is it?
Probably not.
At least the halls are decked with holly,
Prematurely ripped from a nearby hedgerow.
Not many berries this year because
The bloody birds have eaten them all
And as for mistletoe! I think not.
Too many Christmas days have been sullied

By the over-use of that particular parasite.
But all in all we had a jolly, jolly time,
Didn't we? Well,
Probably not.

The people have spoken

The people have spoken
And the fine, crystal cup of reason
Has been shattered by the dissonant pitch of their ugly voice.
Now the temples are smeared with gratuitous graffiti
And tolerance has turned to hate.
Compassion is compressed under the jackboot
Of nationalist rhetoric,
While the very vocabulary of freedom
Has been dismembered by the dissemblers of democracy.
Promises are fractured and displayed as truths,
Bandaged and supported by splints of deceit.
The full panoply of populism is splurged across red top tabloids
Who urge division and discontent
On a readership, too self-absorbed
By all but the narrow confines of their own lives.
The forces of darkness have been unleashed.
Ignorance and isolationism rule the air-waves
And the drumbeat of xenophobia hammers home
Its message of fear and misunderstanding.
The barbarians are at the gates,
Ready to pillage and burn
Everything that we have learned since the beginning of time.

Oh dear!

There have been times I've been accused,
Some might even say abused.
For spending too much of my time
Composing lines that do not rhyme.

What can I say in my defence,
In future, past or present tense
Except that I, a hapless amateur
Know nothing of the word pentameter.

Iambic is another word
Of which I've scarcely ever heard.
So stupid I'm afraid, but then
Could be a statement of a pen.

Another problem that I find
Concerns the word Alexandrine.
Perhaps someone could help me out
And tell me what that's all about.

Hang on a sec, whispers my muse
Hexameter's the word we use.
Dodecosyllable will suffice
But I don't think that's very nice.

For some it might work out just fine
But you try and fit it in a six beat line.
Spenserian forms are just not me
Nor, I think, will ever be.

And so for better or for worse
I think I'll stick to free-er verse.
Because it's plain I have no time
To search for lines that scan and rhyme.

About the author

John Hallam Lott has a degree in, and a deep love of, history. He has written short stories for radio, is a prize-winning poet and is currently working on his second novel.

John lives with his wife, an artist, in a particularly beautiful region of Northern France and does much of his thinking and planning while walking the surrounding countryside and, from time to time, some of the sunnier parts of Europe.

By the same author:

Designed to Deceive
by John Hallam Lott

1077, Dover Castle – William 1st, King of England and Duke of Normandy is captivated by the presence of a stranger in the Great Hall. This young man does not know himself why he has been summoned or by whom. Nor could he guess how his incredible talents will be employed in the ensuing weave of murder, deceit and betrayal.

FICTION / HISTORICAL

Also available from WebVivant Press:

FICTION

Lady Caine
The weird side of the War on Drugs
by Steve Mansfield-Devine

A strange cast of misfits is on the hunt for a missing pilot – either for what he has or what he knows. Each member of this weird posse poses a threat to the others. But their greatest danger comes from their own egos, paranoia, incompetence and inability to cope. The result is an offbeat thriller about the hilarious fringes of international drug crime.

FICTION / CRIME / COMEDY / THRILLER

Black Project
Nothing is beyond belief
by Steve Mansfield-Devine

In this darkly funny novel, a tabloid journalist and an engineer engaged on classified government black projects come into contact with a strange secret. It both realizes their dreams and confirms their nightmares. It's a story of paranoia, weird conspiracies, an out of control government and people pushed to the edge of understanding.

FICTION / SATIRE / COMEDY / THRILLER

Twisting Tales
From the everday to a world of disconcerting magic
by Clare Le May

In *Twisting Tales*, Clare Le May gives us a collection of gems. Mixing fantasy and the everyday. These short stories are a deceptively light read that is no lightweight experience

FICTION / SHORT STORIES / DRAMA

*

NON-FICTION

Make Do & Cook

Learn the secrets of 10 important foods and how to cook healthy, delicious meals on the smallest budget

by Patricia Mansfield-Devine

Make Do & Cook teaches you how you can eat well on a budget. Whether you're a student, a pensioner or a parent with a family to feed, this is your guide to making tasty, cheap and nutritious meals without spending hours in the kitchen. It includes chapters on savvy shopping, menu planning and budgeting, essential ingredients and 100 simple and delicious recipes.

NON-FICTION / COOKING / FOOD

For more information, go to: www.webvivantpress.com

www.ingramcontent.com/pod-product-compliance
Lightning Source LLC
Chambersburg PA
CBHW020527030426
42337CB00011B/568